John Muir:
Protector of the Wilderness

by Kristin Cashore

Scott Foresman
is an imprint of

Glenview, Illinois • Boston, Massachusetts • Chandler, Arizona
Upper Saddle River, New Jersey

Every effort has been made to secure permission and provide appropriate credit for photographic material. The publisher deeply regrets any omission and pledges to correct errors called to its attention in subsequent editions.

Unless otherwise acknowledged, all photographs are the property of Scott Foresman, a division of Pearson Education.

Photo locators denoted as follows: Top (T), Center (C), Bottom (B), Left (L), Right (R), Background (Bkgd)

Opener: Library of Congress, Getty Images; 3 Brand X Picture, Corbis, Getty Images; 4 Getty Images; 5 Getty Images; 6 Getty Images; 7 Getty Images; 8 Getty Images; 9 Getty Images; 11 Getty Images; 12 Getty Images; 13 Getty Images, Digital Vision; 14–15 Digital Vision; 16 Digital Vision; 17 Digital Vision; 18 (R) Quarter-dollar coin image from the U.S. Mint/Digital Vision; 19 Digital Vision; 20 Brand X Pictures; 21 Brand X Pictures; 22 Getty Images

ISBN 13: 978-0-328-51635-3
ISBN 10:   0-328-51635-X

3 4 5 6 7 8 9 10 V0N4 13 12 11 10

A Preserver Among the Settlers

Imagine a beautiful land with forests and hills, lakes and rivers, and lots of wildlife. The land has plenty of wood to build houses, plenty of land to farm, plenty of animals for food, and plenty of water. But what happens if we start to cut down the trees for houses? What happens when our cows begin to eat all of the grass on the hills? What if we need to dam the river to gather water and make electricity? What if we drive the animals away?

When people settle a new place, the landscape must change. In the nineteenth century, the American West was a wilderness, and people moved in to "tame" it. As a result, our country prospered and grew. At the same time, the environment changed.

Many people were full of ideas about how they could use the American West. Only a few people realized what Americans were doing to the American West. Only a few were thinking about the land, the plants, the animals, and the trees. One of those people was John Muir.

John Muir

An American Hero from Scotland

John Muir may have spent his life fighting to **preserve** America's natural wonders, but he was not an American. Muir was born in Dunbar, Scotland, on April 21, 1838. Even as a young boy, he loved the outdoors. Whenever Muir could sneak away from his schoolwork, he walked along the Scottish coast and wandered through the countryside. When he was eleven years old, his life changed. His family moved to the United States.

A street banner that honors John Muir in the town of Dunbar

The Scottish coast near Muir's childhood home in Dunbar, Scotland

In 1849 the Muir family settled in Wisconsin and started a farm. Until he was twenty-one, Muir spent almost all of his time working on this farm. He did not go to school, but he found time to teach himself math, literature, and other subjects that interested him. Muir developed a skill for building and inventing things. He made working clocks from scratch and even invented a machine that tipped him out of bed in the morning!

Life in Wisconsin was very hard work, and Muir did not have a lot of free time. Whenever he could, though, Muir roamed through the fields and the forests. He loved the outdoors, and even farmwork led him to become an amateur **naturalist,** or person who studies living things.

Muir's home in Wisconsin

The Wanderer Leaves Home

In 1860 Muir left the farm and went to the Wisconsin State Fair in Madison. He took clocks that he had built to the fair, and he won prizes for them!

The next year, Muir studied at the University of Wisconsin. Because he had learned so much on his own, Muir passed a high school program and got right into college. He did very well in his classes and became fascinated with **botany,** the study of plants.

In 1863 Muir left Wisconsin and entered what he called "The University of the Wilderness." He walked all the way from Wisconsin to Mississippi, studying the trees and plants along his path.

John Muir invented and built clocks that kept good time.

For the next few years, Muir explored the northern United States and Canada. While he wandered, he worked odd jobs. In Canada, he worked at a sawmill and a broom and rake factory. In Indiana, he worked at a carriage factory.

In 1867 when Muir was almost thirty years old, there was a terrible accident in the carriage factory. Muir, who had always found the natural world so beautiful, became blind. After a few difficult weeks, his eyesight began to return. It took months for him to recover completely and regain his sight. When he did, he chose to leave his work in the factory.

Muir's accident made him realize that he wanted to spend his life in forests and on mountains, not in factories. He set out on a long walk to Florida. This was the beginning of a lifetime of wandering and study. For the rest of his days, Muir traveled, studied, and learned from the University of the Wilderness.

The University of Wisconsin

California and the World

Where did Muir go? So many places! From Florida, he sailed to New York, Cuba, Panama, and California. He explored California's mountains, valleys, and rivers. He traveled through the American West and made his way to the mountains and **glaciers** of Alaska. He visited the Appalachian Mountains and explored the eastern states. He returned to Alaska many times.

In later years, Muir's wanderings took him to parts of Europe as well as Russia, Korea, Japan, China, India, Egypt, Australia, New Zealand, Indonesia, the Philippines, Hong Kong, and Hawaii. He visited Brazil and Chile, South Africa, and parts of eastern Africa. He went to museums, and he visited the great bridges and buildings that people had built. But it was the natural world that thrilled him; it was the rivers and the forests that he traveled to see.

This is California's Yosemite National Park.

Muir visited many places, but California became his home, and he loved his surroundings. The Sierra Nevada were the most beautiful mountains he had ever seen. Muir did not think anything compared to the valleys, waterfalls, and cliffs of Yosemite.

California is also the home of the giant redwood trees. These trees can grow to be more than three hundred feet tall, with trunks twenty feet wide. Some of the giant redwoods are more than three thousand years old. John Muir loved these trees and always returned to them after his wanderings.

California's redwoods are among the most magnificent trees in the world.

The background shows the Sierra Nevada.

Words Can Save Mountains

But there was no denying it: The acts of humans were harming the Sierra Nevada, Yosemite, and other parts of California. As people settled in California, they chopped down the magnificent redwoods. Muir could not bear to see people destroying nature. So what did he do? He began to write.

Muir wrote articles about animals and plants. He wrote about bees, salmon, sheep, birds, and trees. He wrote about glaciers and earthquakes. Everything in nature interested Muir, and he shared his knowledge by writing it down.

Some of his most important writing was about **conservation.** Muir wrote passionately about saving nature from the carelessness of humans. He fought for the preservation of the redwoods. He wrote about sheep and cows whose grazing was ruining the environments of California. In his writing, Muir begged people to be more careful and to preserve the natural world.

Muir loved writing as much as he loved nature.

Muir also wrote down his own philosophy, or beliefs, about the way the world worked. Muir believed that all living things were connected and that no living thing was more important than any other. A worm was just as important as a human, and all living things worked together to keep Earth healthy. Muir wanted humans to stop acting as if they were more important than other living things. He wanted humans to respect Earth and every **species** on it.

Important magazines started publishing Muir's writings, and people all over the country began to read what Muir had to say. Many people agreed with his ideas and opinions. Because of Muir, people joined the fight to protect nature. Muir began to gain some very powerful friends.

Muir at work in his den

Famous Friends and Allies

Muir's writings caught the attention of many famous people of his time. Asa Gray was a famous professor who studied botany. Gray visited Muir in California, and they traveled and studied together. Gray even named a few plants that he discovered for Muir!

The great philosopher and writer Ralph Waldo Emerson also visited Muir. This was exciting for Muir, who was a fan of Emerson's works. Emerson respected Muir's ideas, and the two men became good friends.

Ralph Waldo Emerson

Asa Gray

Muir's most powerful friend and visitor was the President of the United States, Theodore Roosevelt. President Roosevelt had read Muir's writings and liked what he had to say. Roosevelt wrote a letter to Muir asking Muir to show him the mountains of California.

Muir agreed, and for three days in 1903, John Muir went camping with the President of the United States! They sat under the trees in Yosemite and talked about conservation. Muir explained to President Roosevelt that the wilderness was in danger of being destroyed. He asked the President to help preserve America's natural beauty. He stressed that the mountains and forests were important to all people.

President Roosevelt and many others took Muir's message seriously, and because of Muir, the country began to change.

In 1903 John Muir showed President Roosevelt the natural beauty of California.

Muir Creates the National Park System

President Roosevelt left the mountains of California and returned to the White House, but he did not forget the beauty of California. He did not forget what Muir had said about conserving nature.

While Roosevelt was president he started the U.S. Forest Service, which works to protect our forests. He created 150 national forests, five national parks, eighteen national monuments, and fifty-one new wildlife refuges. Today President Theodore Roosevelt is famous for conservation. Without his actions, many of our most beautiful lands might not exist.

Muir did not stop after encouraging the President. He continued to write long articles explaining that lands should be protected, and he worked hard to educate people about conservation. He fought for the creation of national parks.

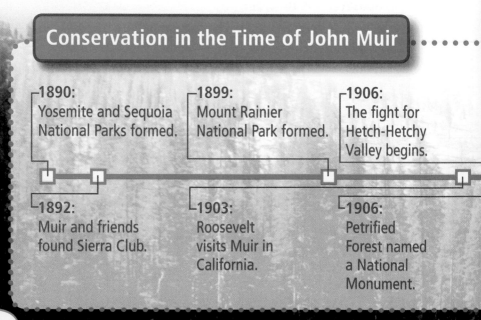

Conservation in the Time of John Muir

1890: Yosemite and Sequoia National Parks formed.

1899: Mount Rainier National Park formed.

1906: The fight for Hetch-Hetchy Valley begins.

1892: Muir and friends found Sierra Club.

1903: Roosevelt visits Muir in California.

1906: Petrified Forest named a National Monument.

Muir's hard work led to the creation of Yosemite National Park and Sequoia National Park in California and Mount Rainier National Park in Washington. It also led to the protection of the Petrified Forest and the Grand Canyon in Arizona. Muir's writing was so important and influential that today he is often called the father of our national park system.

In 1892 Muir and some of his followers decided to start an organization to preserve the Sierra Nevada. They called this organization the Sierra Club, and Muir served as its president from 1892 to 1914. Muir wrote that the Sierra Club would "do something for wilderness and make the mountains glad." Today the Sierra Club continues working to preserve nature and educate people all over the world.

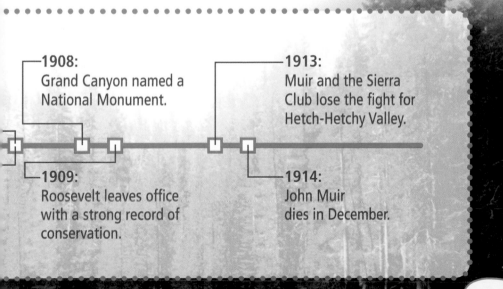

1908:
Grand Canyon named a National Monument.

1909:
Roosevelt leaves office with a strong record of conservation.

1913:
Muir and the Sierra Club lose the fight for Hetch-Hetchy Valley.

1914:
John Muir dies in December.

One Last Fight

In the later years of Muir's life, he spent time with his wife and two daughters and wrote even more than he had earlier. During his life he published more than three hundred articles and ten books. He never stopped traveling the world, and he never stopped fighting for the cause of conservation.

Unfortunately, Muir did not always win his fights. One of his greatest disappointments involved the Hetch-Hetchy Valley in Yosemite. The Hetch-Hetchy Valley was a gorgeous part of Yosemite through which the Tuolumne River flowed.

The Tuolumne River dam

Yosemite's Hetch-Hetchy Valley

In 1906 there was an earthquake in San Francisco and a fire destroyed most of the city. After the earthquake, city officials decided that they wanted to dam the Tuolumne River and flood the Hetch-Hetchy Valley. This would create a reservoir of water to supply San Francisco. It would also make it easier to put fires out the next time there was an earthquake.

John Muir and the Sierra Club battled to protect the Hetch-Hetchy Valley from the city's decision. The fierce fight lasted seven years. In 1913 President Woodrow Wilson signed a bill that gave the city of San Francisco the right to dam the Tuolumne River and flood the Hetch-Hetchy Valley. Muir and the Sierra Club had lost the fight, and the world had lost the valley.

The fight against damming of the Tuolumne River and flooding of the Hetch-Hetchy Valley was Muir's last battle. One year later, while visiting one of his daughters in Los Angeles, he caught pneumonia. At the age of seventy-six, John Muir died, but this lover and protector of our country's wilderness has not been forgotten.

The Tuolumne River

Muir's Legacy

John Muir was one of our country's most important naturalists. Millions of people have read his books. His writing has changed people's attitudes. It is thanks to John Muir and others like him that many Americans today care about nature and the environment. People who work toward conservation today are acting in the spirit of John Muir.

John Muir is so admired that many parks, trails, and organizations are named after him. The John Muir Trust is a Scottish organization that works to protect the environment. The Muir Woods National Monument is a forest of protected redwood trees in California. The John Muir Trail runs for 211 miles through some of the most beautiful mountains in California. The John Muir Wilderness is a large area in California full of mountains, lakes, and streams. The Sierra Club has also grown over the years, and today it does important conservation work all over the world.

The California quarter and some stamps have John Muir's image on them.

Quarter-dollar coin image from the U.S. Mint

18

Even Muir's Hetch-Hetchy Valley is still an open question. Today the Sierra Club is working to reverse the Hetch-Hetchy Valley decision. It wants to empty the dam and return the river and the valley to their original state. In the meantime, the Sierra Club works to prevent other destructive dams from being built.

The Muir Woods National Monument in California is named after John Muir.

Muir Opens America's Eyes

In the nineteenth century, America was full of settlers. Many of these settlers saw mountains, trees, and valleys as an opportunity to build homes, farms, and towns. These settlers weren't worried about the trees they cut down or the animals they drove away. They didn't realize how much America had to lose. It took a young man from Scotland to see these same mountains, trees, and valleys as national treasures.

Nature was John Muir's escape from a hard day's work on the farm, and it was his comfort after a scary eye injury. Nature taught him at the University of the Wilderness. Nature showed him one of life's truths: All living things, no matter how big or small, are important. Muir knew the value of nature, and he made nature the work of his lifetime. It took him a lifetime of work to open America's eyes to its own beauty.

If you ever have a chance to visit a national park, remember John Muir. Our country's natural wonders might not be here today if Muir had not seen them and loved them. Our wilderness might have disappeared long ago if Muir had not defended it.

Yosemite National Park

Now Try This

Be a Settler and a Conserver

It is your turn to conserve nature! Often when a house is built, the land around the house is cleared. Trees are chopped down, shrubs are uprooted, and weeds and other plants are removed. After the house is built, the owners may plant grass, but the wild growth from before is lost. Insects and animals are pushed away. But there are ways to bring the wildness back. Take charge of this conservation effort and see what you can do to restore what has been lost!

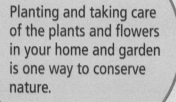

Planting and taking care of the plants and flowers in your home and garden is one way to conserve nature.

1. First, you need to decide what changes you will make. What things lived and grew here before your home was built? What kinds of trees, shrubs, and flowers would you like to plant? Do you want to include any bird feeders? A fountain or pond? A bee hive? Make a list!

2. Next, make a plan. Where will you get the materials you need? How will you learn the steps involved in planting a tree or caring for a garden? How will you learn to garden in ways that are good for the environment? Make a list of the questions you will need to ask in order to complete your plan.

3. Draw a rough diagram of how your yard will look when you have planted your trees and plants. Where will each tree go? Which flowers will go in which garden? Where will you hang the bird feeders?

4. Plan for the future. Will you plant more trees later on? Will you plant the same flowers every year? How can you continue to encourage birds, squirrels, spiders, and other creatures to use your yard as their home?

Glossary

botany *n.* the science of plants; study of plants and plant life.

conservation *n.* preservation from harm or decay; protection from loss or from being used up.

glaciers *n.* great masses of ice moving very slowly down a mountain, along a valley, or over a land area.

naturalist *n.* a person who makes a study of living things.

preserve *v.* to keep from harm or change; keep safe; protect.

species *n.* a set of related living things that all have certain characteristics.